MORE THAN JUST A DOG, MY DOG IS

AF597028

HOW TO BE YOUR DOG'S BEST FRIEND EVEN WHEN YOU ARE BUSY WORKING

JAMES SCOTT

Copyright©2022 Authors Name

All Rights Reserved

Table of Contents

INTRODUCTION

Dogs may significantly improve the lives of their owners. They affect children's social, emotional, and cognitive growth, encourage an active lifestyle, offer companionship, and have even been used to spot cancer or impending epileptic episodes.

The most devoted animals with four legs are dogs. They behave when they feel a connection to their people or when they are in danger. A dog will protect your home and those you love, one of the most valuable benefits of owning one.

So how do you get bonded with your dog? How do you become best of friends?

CHAPTER 1

Is owning a dog good for you?

You may live longer if you have a dog. A thorough analysis of papers released between 1950 and 2019 revealed that dog owners had a decreased mortality risk. According to studies, people who own dogs have lower blood pressure and better reactions to stress.

Affection and company. Puppy love is the name given to it for a reason. There are few experiences in life that can compare to being greeted by a happy dog, replete with a wagging tail and lolling tongue, as you enter the house after a demanding day at work. Dogs are tremendously devoted, eager to please, and generous with their affection. Never undervalue the power of the bond you can form with your dog,

Various breeds for various personalities. Similar to people, dogs have a wide range of personality types. While some dogs are eager to participate in athletic competitions, swims, or treks, others are satisfied to cuddle with their human friends for extended periods of time. Whatever your interests and lifestyle may be, there is probably a dog out there that would be the ideal match.

Instill responsibility in children. If your kids have been pleading with you for a pet, now could be the ideal time to instill in them the value of responsibility. Even young children are capable of helping with feeding, grooming, and walking the family pet; dogs need a lot of love and care.

Getting off on a new start.

Numerous adorable puppies develop into adult dogs with uncontrollable behavioral issues, and animal shelters are crowded with dogs that were abandoned because no one bothered to train them. Training should be your main priority if you want your puppy to develop into the adult dog you've always wanted. Puppies can learn at any age, so your training sessions should begin the day your new family member arrives.

It's simple to fall in love with your new puppy thanks to features like their satiny smooth ears, exquisitely plump paw pads, and adorable puppy dog eyes. However, what you teach your new puppy is a completely different matter.

A dog bed, mat, or crate are the finest options if you want to give your new puppy a location that is exclusively his or hers. In order for your dog to understand that the best things happen when they are in their place, regardless of what is going on around them, you should teach them the "place" command.

Potty training should also come first on your list of lessons to educate your new dog in order to protect your flooring. Before beginning, you should think about your living conditions and your puppy's immunization schedule, but the basic three steps for potty training a dog never change.

Next, you should learn what to do if your dog makes a mistake, which they will unavoidably do. If you see your puppy squatting or lifting a leg on the carpet, gently stop them and take them outdoors to their designated pee area. Unfortunately, the only thing you can do is grab the carpet cleaner if you don't catch them in the act and only discover the foul proof of their crime. It won't help you to scold them after the fact or rub their nose in the mud; in fact, doing so will severely harm your developing friendship.

Last but not least, manage your expectations. The conventional consensus is that pups can only "hold it" for as long as they are a month old. So, every two hours, your two-month-old puppy will need to use the restroom.

Show your puppy where to use the bathroom first. Say something like, "Go potty," and give them praise when they use the restroom.

Suitable Playing.

A puppy that plays bites can be adorable, but the issue will get worse as the dog ages. Teach your new puppy appropriate play beginning with your first play session in order to give it the best chance of success. If they play with their fangs or claws, stop them right away and exclaim in a shocked tone of voice something like, "Ouch!"

They won't pick up the "no teeth" lesson right away, but if you persist, they will ultimately see the connection and understand that if they bite, the pleasure is over. Never forget that training a puppy with harsh punishment never works.

CHAPTER 2

Do dogs choose a best friend?

Can dogs form friendships? They can, a key characteristic that sets them apart from wolves.

Despite the fact that most of the data are still based on observations, it appears that dogs occasionally select their best pals, whether they are other dogs, other animals, or humans. The domestication and socialization of dogs by humans may have increased their capacity for companionship as well.

How do I show my dogs friendship?

Spend quality time with your dog

Spending time together will build your connection because a relationship is about being with one another and exchanging experiences, especially if you do so in enjoyable ways. Try going on a walk and spending some quality time playing with your dog.

Train your dog.

Puppies who are well-trained are given more freedom. They can spend more time off-leash if they respond to the call of the owner. They can hang around throughout meals if they choose not to eat what is on the table. Training also lessens frustration since your dog will know exactly what you want when you ask them to do something they have been taught to do.

Study up on dog behavior.

Particularly stressed-out body language and facial gestures. It's simpler for you to protect or remove your dog from uncomfortable circumstances when you can recognize the symptoms of anxiety or fear in them. The trust between you and your dog will improve if they can depend on you to keep them safe, which will also strengthen your relationship.

Clear communication is essential.

Misunderstandings and misunderstandings are the enemies of good relationships, so speak with your dog as clearly as possible. Maintain consistency in your training cues. Because dogs acquire visual cues faster than vocal cues, use the former whenever available. Dogs pay more attention to what you do than what you say, so pay attention to what you do while communicating with them. When you and your partner have a better understanding of each other, you will feel closer.

Be playful.

Scientists have noticed that in a variety of species, parents who play with their kids have the closest relationships with them; it also appears that this is true in interactions between people and dogs. Togetherness is strengthened by having fun and playing games.

Socializing.

The process of socialization involves getting a dog or cat ready to enjoy interactions and feel at ease with other animals, people, locations, and activities. The "sensitive phase," which is between 3 and 14 weeks of age for pups and 3 and 9 weeks of age for kittens, is the ideal time for socializing to start.

Why it's important to socialize your dog

Through socialization, your dog learns how to respond to the world in a healthy way, devoid of needless fear or violence. Starting early can help you, and your dog avoids additional difficulties.

The American Veterinary Society of Animal Behavior claims that behavioral problems, not infectious diseases, are the leading cause of death in young dogs.

How to socialize your dog.

Daily walks are essential. Simply taking your dog for a stroll in a public area will help him become more accustomed to the surroundings and the people there.

More than just introducing your new puppy to other canines and humans is necessary for socialization.

It's important to expose your puppy to various sights, noises, and textures. It also helps to get your puppy to play with a variety of individuals and allow kids to play with it in a controlled environment.

Be sure to socialize your puppy gradually and respect your puppy's boundaries. Make conversations enjoyable by showering them with praise and treats. Your puppy is still learning everything, so every interaction is a chance to establish a good connection.

When exposing your puppy to adult canines, try not to overexert yourself because the puppy will sense it. Take small steps and avoid attempting to accomplish too much at once. Introduce people cautiously; if your puppy feels overwhelmed, it can later respond fearfully in huge crowds or other situations.

How do you fix a badly socialized dog?

If you believe your dog needs more socialization, investing in some training is the greatest thing you can do to help. Start by making sure your dog is familiar with fundamental commands like "heel," "sit," and "come," all of which can be useful if your dog begins to misbehave. But spending time socializing with your dog is even better.

All canines, regardless of age, can be socialized. You can try socializing your dog on your own if you're up for it. This is more suitable for dogs who are just a little bit frightened. Professional dog trainers are better equipped to handle the socialization of dogs who are extremely scared or aggressive.

When your dog overreacts, the worst thing you can do is support his response by acting in a similar way. Your dog takes your panic as your approval of their response to the circumstance.

CHAPTER 3

What is reward in dog training?

Reward-based training is precisely what it sounds like, and it's frequently referred to as "positive reinforcement training." By rewarding desired actions with items your dog enjoys, you can train your dog to perform the behavior you want.

It may appear easy to use treats as a kind of reinforcement for your dog when you urge it to mimic a certain action. But adequately rewarding your dog is actually an art.

Rewards' significance.

A reward is used in positive reinforcement training to encourage desirable actions. Positive reinforcement is one of your most effective methods for modifying or shaping your dog's behavior since it increases their likelihood of repeating the behavior for the reward.

Timing your reward

To ensure that your dog understands and can duplicate the cue, timing your reward is essential.

Dogs also lack the ability to link events from the past with one another. The majority of trainers agree that you only have around 1.3 seconds to treat a dog successfully; otherwise, the behavior won't get associated with the incentive.

If you don't give your dog a reward right away, they can link it with totally other activities. This can be seen during house training, for instance. Many people praise house-trained dogs when they return inside after going outside to urinate or defecate, but this only praises the dog for returning inside, not for going outside to urinate or defecate. As long as they respond when called, your puppy may still believe the world is their potty despite your best efforts at housebreaking them. You should go outside with your potty-

training dog and give them a treat as soon as they urinate to genuinely reinforce the behavior.

You can start cutting back on the rewards once your dog routinely goes outdoors and doesn't have any accidents.

Reward with dog treat.

The majority of expert dog trainers advise dog owners to start their dogs' obedience training with tasty goodies and later wean them off of them. Although it is possible to educate your dog without treats, starting with food rewards ensures that you have their full attention. Treats are an effective training technique. With goodies, your dog will pick things up more rapidly.

Other ways to rewarding your dog without treat

Using goodies could also make your dog obsess over them rather than engage in the desired activity. This might even result in begging.

Fortunately, there are other approaches to rewarding your dog that doesn't include giving them treats. Here are some substitute methods for rewarding your dog while forgoing the treats.

- Measure food, cuddle, play with a favorite or new toy, and more.
- *Verbal Gratitude.*
- *Using a brush.*
- *Using a clicker to train.*
- *Time for general play or exercise.*
- *A visit to the canine park or a fresh walking route*

CHAPTER 4

Care for your dog.

Pets, like people, require food that specifically fulfills their nutritional requirements. Both dog and cat diets are made to satisfy the nutritional requirements of the respective species. They have quite diverse dietary needs, which is important. Puppies and older dogs demand different foods. Pets with medical conditions could need specific diets. Table scraps are generally not a good idea for dogs and cats because many of the foods we eat, like salt, garlic, and onions, are unhealthy for pets and can cause them to become ill or even die.

Pets should receive the appropriate amount of food, too. Giving your pet too many treats or overfeeding him might make him obese, which can bring on additional health issues like heart disease and kidney issues. To prevent these ailments, weigh your alternatives when it comes to pet food. If you're unsure of which meals would be best for your pet, it's a wonderful idea to ask your veterinarian for advice.

Pets, like people, require easy access to water in order to survive. Always provide every animal under your care with a clean, fresh dish of water. Remember to restock your pet's water dish at least twice a day and make it accessible by positioning it close to their food bowl. Your pet will stay cool, hydrated, and healthy as a result.

Aquariums should be cleaned at least once every week if your pet is an aquatic animal like fish or a turtle. Inaction could result in unhealthy animals and odorous tanks!

Exercise is an essential component of proper pet care. Exercise is crucial for both the physical and mental wellness of your cat. If you spend time on social media, you probably already know that various kinds of animals enjoy playing, like this turtle who is bouncing a ball, this dog who is playing fetch by himself, or this bird that is playing with a red cup. Some people mistake what they see as a pet's misbehavior for the animal simply being bored and enjoying itself by going into the trash, destroying the couch, or, well, you get the point. Looking for ideas on how to spend time with your dog?

Whether through frequent engagement with you, having visitors over, or going out, pets can benefit from socialization. While assisting them in safety, experiencing new things, broadening their horizons, and enhancing their interpersonal skills!

You should take your pets for wellness check-ups at least once a year to a reputable local veterinarian to make sure they are strong and agile. It's important to keep your pet's vaccines current. Your pet's health also greatly benefits from having clean teeth and healthy gums. Take your animal companion to the vet or animal hospital as soon as possible if they are exhibiting sickly signs or symptoms so that they can recover more quickly.

Regular grooming is another approach to keep your pets happy and healthy (if needed). For dogs, matted fur can be uncomfortable and unhealthy. Although washes, brushings, nail trimmings, and flea/tick removal may be required for your pet's health, dogs and cats may not enjoy it.

You and your cherished pet are well on your way to a lifetime of happiness, together with the aforementioned advice on basic pet care!

Ways to take care of your dog while working.

You have fantastic work, a terrific social life, and encouraging family and friends, yet something is still lacking. Can I acquire a dog if I work all day? You've always loved dogs and would do anything to have your very own furry child to care for. Having a dependent dog in your home seems unjust, especially if you plan to spend the entire day at work.

Although having a dog and a full-time job may not be for everyone, it is possible to make it work if you're open to trying a few different approaches to ensure everyone's requirements are satisfied. These are a few ways to care for a dog or puppy while you are working. If you're keen about adopting, then buy a new dog or puppy but are concerned about your work commitments.

This advice won't help you if you already have a dog. But if you're thinking of adopting a dog and you're asking, "Should I have a dog if I work all day?" one of the greatest things you can do is do your homework on different dog breeds and pick one that is most likely to react well to being left alone for the majority of the day while you're at work. Some dog breeds are more dependent on human interaction than others; therefore, when left alone during the day, they are more likely to feel separation anxiety. Other dog breeds are more independent and can tolerate long periods alone without issue.

There are some situations when you might be able to bring your dog to work with you, but this advice won't apply to everyone. You might be able to answer the issue, "What should I do with my puppy when I go to work?" by just bringing your dog or puppy along with you if you work outside, in a family-friendly atmosphere, or spend a lot of time driving your own car as part of your employment.

Give your dog a vigorous exercise session before you leave for work if you intend for them to sleep peacefully throughout the day while you are at work. To enhance the likelihood that your dog will spend most of the day napping and relaxing, make a commitment to spending a significant amount of time engaging in high-energy play or running in addition to their regular morning walk.

If having a dog and working from 9 to 5 worries you, consider making plans to return home during your lunch break. Even if the trip there and back only gives you a brief window of time, it will be enough to check in on your dog, let them out for a bathroom break, refill their food and water bowls, and engage in a small game to let them release some steam before being left alone again after lunch. If you don't have time to eat during this break, try eating later in the day while at your desk or during the commute.

More and more businesses are growing amenable to the concept of allowing workers to work remotely one or more days per week. Focus on the advantages for the business, such as increased productivity, office space liberation, and a decreased use of corporate resources, when talking to your manager about the possibility of working from home.

A dog schedule for working owners can be made if you live with family, friends, or roommates and try to coordinate your schedules. If at all feasible, change your lunch break or working hours to prevent leaving your dog home alone for extended periods of time. If you work near home, taking a later or earlier lunch than normal may result in multiple trips home by human family members, interrupting your dog's day.

When your new puppy first joined your small family, do you remember how much fun you had introducing them? If your job schedule requires you to spend a lot of time apart from your dog, you'll enjoy a joyful reunion each time you two cross paths. When you can finally appreciate spending quality time with your dog again, you'll discover that you look forward to some peaceful time at home. Avoid leaving your dog alone in the evenings and on the weekends if you spend a lot of time apart during the week.

Plan activities that incorporate your dog, such as bringing them along when you go out with friends or having your groceries delivered to your home rather than spending the majority of your Saturday at a mall. Even better, go shopping with your dog in tow at a farmers market that welcomes dogs.

SUMMARY

One of the most significant relationships you will ever have is with your dog, if not the most important one. The foundation for other relationships, such as those between people, animals, and the environment, can be laid by having a fulfilling and positive relationship with your dog.

Your dog's company can provide solace and reduce your anxiety. Numerous studies have demonstrated the calming effects of therapy dogs and dogs in general. Blood pressure, heart rate, breathing rate, and muscle stress are all reduced by simply touching a familiar dog.

Our canine friends give us unconditional affection and support, which lessens our loneliness. Dogs also motivate us to get up and walk about. The extra exercise can benefit our physical health, whether we're walking around the block with our best buddy or discovering a new route.

Apply these steps and see the effect of building a good with your dog

www.ingramcontent.com/pod-product-compliance
Lightning Source LLC
LaVergne TN
LVHW052110160826
845678LV00015B/3465

* 9 7 9 8 8 4 6 4 3 7 3 0 2 *